Agree

Over the past twenty-five years Owen McCafferty's plays have been performed worldwide and have won numerous awards. Previous work includes *Titanic: Scenes from the British Wreck Commissioner's Inquiry, 1912* (MAC, Belfast); *The Absence of Women* (Lyric Theatre, Belfast, and Tricycle Theatre, London); *Days of Wine and Roses* (Donmar Theatre, London); *Closing Time* (National Theatre, London); *Shoot the Crow* (Druid, Galway); *Mojo Mickybo* (Kabosh, Belfast); *Scenes from the Big Picture* (National Theatre, London), which won the Meyer-Whitworth, John Whiting and Evening Standard Awards; *Quietly* (Abbey Theatre, Dublin), which won the Writers' Guild Award for Best Play; *Death of a Comedian* (Abbey Theatre, Dublin, Lyric Theatre, Belfast, and Soho Theatre, London); and *Fire Below* (*A War of Words*) (Lyric Theatre, Belfast, and Abbey Theatre, Dublin). Owen's first screenplay *Ordinary Love* won Best Picture 2020 at the Irish Film & Television Awards.

OWEN McCAFFERTY

Agreement

faber

First published in 2023
by Faber and Faber Limited
74–77 Great Russell Street, London WC1B 3DA

Typeset by Brighton Gray
Printed and bound in the UK by CPI Group (Ltd), Croydon CR0 4YY

A CIP record for this book
is available from the British Library

ISBN 978–0–571–38508–9

2 4 6 8 10 9 7 5 3 1

For Gwyneth

Agreement was commissioned by MGC (the Michael Grandage Company) and produced by the Lyric Theatre, Belfast. It was first performed at the Lyric Theatre, Belfast, on 29 March 2023, with the following cast in alphabetical order:

Senator George Mitchell Richard Croxford
John Hume Dan Gordon
Mo Mowlam Andrea Irvine
Bertie Ahern Ronan Leahy
Gerry Adams Packy Lee
David Trimble Patrick O'Kane
Tony Blair Rufus Wright

Director Charlotte Westenra
Set & Costume Designer Conor Murphy
Lighting Designer Mary Tumelty
Sound Designer & Composer Kate Marlais
Video Designer Eoin Robinson
Movement Director Dylan Quinn
Dialect Coach Brendan Gunn
Percussionist Ruairi Glasheen

Characters

George Mitchell
sixty-four

Tony Blair
forty-four

Gerry Adams
forty-nine

Bertie Ahern
forty-six

David Trimble
fifty-three

John Hume
sixty-one

Mo Mowlam
forty-eight

President Clinton
(*voice-over*)

Newsreader
(*voice-over*)

Time and Place

Tuesday 7th to Friday 10th April 1998
Castle Buildings, Stormont, Belfast, Northern Ireland

AGREEMENT

George Mitchell sets out tables and chairs for the talks.
During this the stage is flooded with images of violence from
the conflict.

Mitchell   (*to audience*) nothing is agreed until everything is
                agreed

        Mo Mowlam, Gerry Adams, David Trimble and
        John Hume enter and take their seats.

        (*To audience.*) april seventh 1998 – castle buildings
        stormont belfast northern ireland – three days left –
        the tail end of peace negotiations – but first some
        background – northern ireland was created in
        1921 – a devolved government for the six most
        northeastern counties of ireland – antrim –
        armagh – derry stroke londonderry – that alone
        gives you a brief insight into the problem –
        nationalists derry unionists londonderry – the
        names of things matter here – fermanagh tyrone
        and down – violence has been ever present since the
        creation of northern ireland – but most intensely
        since the late 1960s – the situation is complex –
        northern ireland is part of the united kingdom –
        unionists stroke loyalists want to maintain that
        union – nationalists stroke republicans want to
        unite with the republic of ireland – and then you
        have the forces of the state – the police and the
        army – a melting pot – i'm senator george
        mitchell – appointed by president bill clinton as
        chairman of these negotiations – sixty-four years
        old – if i were to describe what i do i'd say –
        i simultaneously juggle knives and balloons – so –

the talkers – the decision makers – one last thing –
nothing is agreed until everything is agreed

Mowlam (*to audience*) mo mowlam – northern ireland
secretary of state – i am the british government's
point of view – plain speaking – forty-eight years
old – for the last few years i have been
undergoing treatment for a brain tumour

*She looks at the men around her. She indicates to
John Hume it is his turn. He stands.*

Hume (*to audience*) john hume – social democratic and
labour party – sixty-one years old – an irish
nationalist – a socialist – a pacifist

He sits. David Trimble stands.

Trimble (*to audience*) david trimble – fifty-three years
old – ulster unionist party – i am british – i am
here to maintain the union between great britain
and northern ireland

*David Trimble sits down and Gerry Adams
stands up.*

Adams (*to audience*) gerry adams – forty-nine years old –
sinn fein – belfast man – an irish republican –
a socialist – an irish citizen – my goal is to see the
reunification of my country

Trimble (*to audience*) a leading member of the murderous
ira since the 1970s who i will not deal with

Adams (*to audience*) an elected politician whose
legitimate voice will not be ignored

Adams sits. Mitchell hands them each a document.

There are two documents left which he sets aside.

Mitchell (*to audience; holding up a document*) the mitchell
agreement – not my idea to call it that – (*As he
speaks he flicks through the document.*)

Hume	(*to audience*) strand one – democratic political institutions in northern ireland – a devolved power sharing assembly
Mowlam	(*to audience*) strand two – north south ministerial council – northern irish bodies and southern bodies that could implement practical economic cooperation
Trimble	(*to audience*) strand three – east west relations – a british irish council and a british intergovernmental conference
Adams	(*to audience*) there are also decisions to be made about prisoner release
Trimble	(*to audience*) and disarmament
Hume	(*to audience*) this can only be about one thing – a shared and just future for all citizens
Adams	(*to audience*) the men and women who fought for freedom from british rule must be released
Trimble	(*to audience*) the acceptance of this agreement as far as i am concerned is the end of the debate – northern ireland is british and will remain so
Hume	(*to audience*) as long as the majority of people wish it so
Trimble	(*to audience*) they will always wish it so
Adams	(*to audience*) it is only a matter of time before there is a majority for a united ireland
Hume	(*to audience*) there is a european dimension to this
Trimble	(*to audience*) there is no european dimension there is only a british dimension
Adams	(*to audience*) the north of ireland
Trimble	(*to audience*) northern ireland
Adams	(*to audience*) the north of ireland

Trimble	(*to audience*) northern ireland
Hume	(*to audience*) we are in the european union
Trimble	(*to audience*) we are in northern ireland
Hume	(*to audience*) a rock belongs to no one
Trimble	(*to audience*) land belongs to people – this is our land – it belongs to us and we are british
Adams	(*to audience*) this is the island of ireland – it belongs to the irish
Hume	(*to audience*) we live in a shared space
Mitchell	(*to audience*) and there you have it folks that's what this is all about

Trimble Hume and Adams read the document. Mitchell and Mowlam wait.

(*To audience.*) in over thirty years of conflict more than three thousand people have lost their lives and countless other thousands have been physically injured – the emotional damage has yet to be fully understood – this is what is at stake – peace – regarding the talks themselves there is one person missing – ian paisley – the leader of the democratic unionist party – who decided to walk because of the issue of guns and the release of prisoners – needless to say he is welcome back at any time –

Everyone nods their head in agreement.

one last thing – the weather – it is a dirty day – wet bleak grey – hopefully that isn't an omen – sorry one other last thing – nothing is agreed until everything is agreed

They all quickly flick through the document. They surround Mitchell.

Trimble	(*to Mitchell*) it's a bad paper – a very bad paper – too much interference from the south – a foreign power meddling in our business – unacceptable
Hume	(*to Mitchell*) don't let the unionists mess with strand two
Trimble	(*to Mitchell*) strand two is a huge problem – it is unacceptable
Adams	(*to Mitchell*) concentration on prisoner release is fundamental to our involvement in these talks
Trimble	(*to Mitchell*) these talks will go no further until the irish agree to renegotiate strand two

Silence.

| Mowlam | (*to audience*) so – we're off to a flyer |

Mitchell breaks free from the group.

Mitchell	(*to audience*) then john hume said something to tony blair – who had been keeping himself at arm's length
Hume	(*shouting into phone*) i will not negotiate with a fucking fax machine
Mowlam	(*to audience*) tony thinks this is his moment – flying in to save the day

Tony Blair enters. He lifts a document from the floor and sits on Mo Mowlam's chair. For the rest of the play she has no chair.

| Blair | (*to audience*) for those who don't know – tony blair – forty four years old – prime minister – landslide victory in recent united kingdom elections – i have a huge mandate – (*Aside.*) that's not the first time that's been said to me – a lawyer by trade |

7

Mowlam   (*to audience*) trimble – straight in – one man to another

Trimble   i would like to deal with you directly prime minister rather than the secretary of state

Blair   why

Trimble   because you are the prime minister prime minister

Blair   right – ok – mo

Mowlam   i heard – that's not the reason by the way

Blair   what

Mowlam   trimble thinks i'm too close to the republicans – it would never dawn on him that i'm just doing my job properly – (*To audience.*) anyhoo – back to tony – the messiah

Blair   a lawyer by trade i understand the complexities of negotiations – this irish question is old fashioned – outdated – i can say that . . .

Adams   (*to audience*) he can't say that

Blair   . . . because i'm complex and charismatic

Mowlam   (*to audience*) he's not complex – he's driven – by what and by whom remains to be seen

Mowlam serves tea to Blair and Trimble.

Trimble   prime minister strand two is just unworkable – unworkable – there are too many cross border institutions – the south wants to have too much of a say in what we do

Blair   you are willing to negotiate

Trimble   only if my position is honestly understood

Blair   meaning

Trimble	meaning northern ireland is part of the united kingdom and will be governed as such – that is always the unionist bottom line
Blair	i will talk to irish government and explain the situation – i will act on your behalf
Trimble	i do not doubt that prime minister
Blair	but we are in negotiations – you understand that
Trimble	i understand prime minister

Trimble goes back to his chair. Blair moves to Mowlam.

Blair	what do you think
Mowlam	i think for the time being you need to concentrate on trimble while keeping hume on board and wait and see what adams has to say
Blair	what are you planning on doing
Mowlam	serve tea – you should've told trimble he had to deal with me
Blair	we have no time for that battle
Mowlam	i'm the secretary of state for northern ireland i deserve respect
Blair	i'm the prime minister – (*To audience.*) of everything and everyone
Mowlam	finish your tea prime minister i need to wash your cup

Blair finishes his tea and hands Mowlam the cup. Mitchell takes the cup from Mowlam and pretends to smash it against the wall. Mowlam smiles.

Mitchell	(*to audience*) blair makes a call
Blair	bertie bertie bertie

Bertie Ahern enters and stands apart from the rest.

Ahern	(*to audience*) bertie ahern – forty-six years old – taoiseach – for those of you who can't speak irish and this isn't an exact translation but – irish prime minister – former trade union negotiator – my family history is steeped in republicanism – straightforward and straight talking – someone you could do business with
Blair	bertie
Ahern	tony
Blair	trimble isn't happy
Ahern	what's new
Blair	unless you agree to renegotiate strand two the unionists are going to walk
Ahern	tony removing articles two and three from the irish constitution is not nothing – i'm walking a tightrope here
Trimble	(*to audience*) article two – and three – these have to be removed – the republic of ireland can have no territorial claim to northern ireland – northern ireland is part of the united kingdom – the united kingdom comprising of – england scotland wales and northern ireland – the republic of ireland plays no part in that
Blair	you've freaked the unionists – it was all too much too soon
Ahern	god forbid we should freak the unionists
Blair	at the moment yes
Ahern	pulling back sends the wrong signal
Blair	it sends the right signal
Ahern	i have to think about it
Blair	i know

Trimble	(*to audience*) ahern's mother had died the previous day and her remains were being taken to the catholic chapel that evening
Ahern	(*to audience*) so all eyes on me – after going through the politics of it all i decided not to renegotiate and not to go to stormont tomorrow morning – then i helped carry my mother's coffin into the chapel – death – now i'm walking the streets of dublin trying to work out what to do – trimble isn't going to change his mind – not at the moment anyway – too much pressure on him from his own side – he can't be seen to be weak – you make peace – it isn't handed to you – you negotiate it – peace negotiations – i can't stand in the way of that – i have to try – i can't bury my mother and bury my head – rest in peace mam
Mitchell	it was a big decision by a big man
Trimble	(*to audience*) so ahern has to go to belfast at seven in the morning to meet blair then return to dublin that morning for his mother's funeral after which he has to return to belfast – i admire him for that – don't trust him but i admire him
Hume	(*to audience*) this is the start of the negotiations
Mitchell	(*to audience*) so blair holds a press conference and says
	Cameras clicking and flashing. Microphones descend.
Blair	(*to audience*) this is not a time for sound bites but i feel the hand of history upon my shoulder
	Everyone laughs except Trimble who stands alone.
Trimble	(*shouting over the din*) i won't be railroaded prime minister
	Blair still having his moment with the cameras.

(the din stops during Trimble shouting) i won't be railroaded

Silence.

Blair   i have your back david

Trimble   don't ask me to talk directly with adams

Adams looks at Trimble.

Blair   i know

Trimble   this is a matter of principle

Blair   i know – (*To audience.*) everything here is a matter of principle

Hume and Adams standing within earshot.

Adams   john this is about the people i represent – the people that voted for me – they cannot be ignored – trimble cannot ignore them by ignoring me

Hume   gerry the idea is to get to the end – to reach an agreement – we can't fight every battle

Adams   so once again we negotiate everything on unionist terms

Hume   think of the big picture

Adams   we are all equal – that is the big picture

Hume   it's trimble's last stand

Adams   the people i represent cannot not be ignored

Blair and Trimble are a distance away.

Trimble   none of this is easy

Blair   no – but don't make it harder than it has to be

Trimble   i'm the unionist you want to be dealing with – that doesn't mean i'm any less of a unionist than paisley and his mob shouting from the side lines – if i fail there is a possibility . . .

Blair	we won't fail david – (*To audience.*) i don't fail – or if i do it's certainly not my fault
Trimble	yes prime minister

Blair and Trimble return to their desks. Hume and Adams are moving away from each other.

Hume	i'll report back to you – (*To audience.*) it's not as if the unionists don't know that anyway
Adams	ok – this is about knowing how serious trimble is
Hume	we have to deal with him to find that out gerry
Adams	i have no problem dealing with anyone john

Hume and Adams return to their desks. Mowlam makes sure everyone has tea and then stands beside Mitchell. They have a cup of tea. Mowlam takes her wig off and tosses it on the floor.

Mowlam	too hot
Mitchell	one of the side effects of the medication
Mowlam	one

Everyone drinks tea in silence.

Mitchell	the talks can't run past thursday
Mowlam	they won't – we won't let them – i've been demoted – trimble
Mitchell	tea lady
Mowlam	trimble thinks i'm a spy – thinks i run to adams and hume every time he opens his mouth to me – as if they don't have spies of their own
Mitchell	tony can't push the unionists too hard – trimble has to sell this to moderates while there's an angry crowd behind him baying for blood
Mowlam	he knows that – there's a long way to go – arguing is the main national sport here

Mitchell	world champions at it
Mowlam	hume and trimble have to sit face to face and battle something out – it should be easier when ahern arrives

They laugh.

Everyone finishes their tea.

The sound of a helicopter. Papers are blown everywhere. Everyone on stage gathers them up except Blair. Mitchell puts a small table and two chairs centre stage. Mowlam puts sandwiches and Mars bars on the table. Ahern enters. Everyone stands and bows their heads in silence as a mark of respect. Blair and Ahern sit at the table. Mowlam pours them both a cup of tea, then stands at a distance.

Hume	(*to audience*) another day another weather report – a dirty day – wet bleak grey – no omens there then – the clock – as always – is ticking
Blair	sorry about the circumstances bertie it must be difficult for you
Ahern	it keeps my mind focused
Blair	do you want something to eat – i'm living on sandwiches and mars bars at the moment
Ahern	as tempting as that sounds
Blair	your decision to renegotiate has . . .
Ahern	not renegotiate everything tony
Blair	i understand that bertie – still – your decision has moved everything forward
Ahern	just to be clear tony – trimble can't think he's always pushing an open door
Blair	i understand the situation bertie

Ahern	do you
Blair	i understand perfectly . . .
Ahern	what are you giving up
Blair	we are moving forward
Ahern	in moving forward what are you giving up
Blair	i don't see it like that
Ahern	we're talking about changing my country's constitution – moving from an historic claim to a future aspiration
Blair	i'm putting democracy at the forefront of northern irish politics
Ahern	the point is . . .
Blair	the point is bertie we are both here – this is the time to get this done – this is our time
Ahern	the point is tony – what i am doing isn't nothing – i am willing to do it and i will take whatever flak there is coming to me for doing it – but – trimble must be told there is no triumphalism or grandstanding about this – and you need to tell him he is here to negotiate – it's not a one way street
Blair	he knows that
Ahern	no he doesn't
Blair	he will know it – i need him to talk to hume – i need him to talk to you
Ahern	he'll hate that – thinks the irish are all peasants
Blair	you are all peasants
	They laugh.
Ahern	get him to talk to me face to face – warn him though – i'm not above throwing a punch now and again – you should know that as well

They laugh.

Blair   what about adams

Ahern   it's all about prisoners for him

Blair   he has to be kept on board

Ahern   hume'll do that

Blair   i hear hume's not happy

Ahern   too much attention paid to adams

Blair   he's the one with the guns

Hume   (*to audience*) he's the one with the guns – that's not an easy thing to hear – i've spent my life fighting for civil rights through peaceful protest – i understand the situation – the guns are there – they're not going to magically disappear – they have to be negotiated out of existence – everybody needs to be round the table – i understand that – i'm the one got adams here – i understand it – just not an easy thing to hear – none of this is easy – for any of us – that needs to be understood from the start – everyone at these talks knows that – mightn't always be said but it is certainly known

Ahern   right – i'll be back after the funeral

Blair   and then are you staying here until . . .

Ahern   no – i'll go back and stay the night in my own jurisdiction

Blair   oh right – is that a tactic

Ahern   no – just going home

Blair   i can't fly back to england – home

Ahern   northern ireland is part of your home – you have a residence here

Blair   ah right – of course – forgot about that

They shake hands. Ahern exits. A helicopter takes off and blows papers everywhere. Blair moves back to his seat. Mowlam moves the table and chairs, etc. Trimble enters Blair's 'office'. He immediately starts pacing.

sit down david

Trimble	i have a bad back i can't sit
Blair	i've seen you sit
Trimble	of course i sit prime minister i mean i can't . . .
Blair	have you tried . . .
Trimble	i've tried everything prime minister
Blair	you should take pain killers
Trimble	i do
Blair	i was told by someone who knows that you should never let pain settle – always be ahead of the game
Trimble	talking about pain settling – strand two prime minister
Ahern	(*to audience*) strand two – a north south ministerial council to be established to look into areas of common ground
Adams	(*to audience*) agriculture
Mitchell	(*to audience*) education
Hume	(*to audience*) transport
Mowlam	(*to audience*) environment protection
Adams	(*to audience*) social security and social welfare
Mitchell	(*to audience*) and tourism
Blair	talking about pain – i've talked to bertie and . . .
Trimble	i assume the irish prime minister is pushing too hard prime minister

Blair	never assume – it makes an ass of you and me
Trimble	prime minister
Blair	they are amending their constitution
Trimble	as they should – i need to know that you understand my situation – we at all times must be responsible for our own affairs – imagine france had a say in how you governed your country – his list is too long
Blair	as your prime minister i will negotiate on your behalf as best as i can and as honestly as i can – but – my aim is to get a deal not burn a flag
Trimble	i do not burn flags prime minister – i am walking a tightrope here and there are plenty below me wanting me to fall and plenty more shaking the rope
Blair	i understand
Trimble	do you – i am british – as british as you are
Blair	i know that
Trimble	it's important you do
Blair	we are here to make a deal
Trimble	tell the irish prime minister we will not engage on strand one issues until strand two issues have been addressed – prime minister
Blair	david

Trimble leaves. On his way to his chair he bumps into Mowlam who is pushing a tea trolly.

Mowlam	tea david
Trimble	no thank you secretary of state – the irish are asking for too much – too much
Mowlam	would you like to discuss that david

Trimble i have already made my feelings clear to the prime minister – he is dealing with it

Mowlam (*to audience*) of course he is – why would you let me know your feelings on the issue – i'm only the secretary of state for northern ireland – what possible insight could i have – it's not that i spend my waking day thinking about things like that – that would be ridiculous – what the fuck would i know – i'm only the tea lady

Trimble sits on his chair. Mowlam moves to Adams who is reading the document.

Mowlam would you like a cup of tea gerry

Adams yes thank you mo

She pours him a cup of tea, etc.

Mowlam it makes for good reading

Adams we'll see

Mowlam what are your thoughts

Adams mo – please

Mowlam you must have your own thoughts gerry

Adams whether i do or not is irrelevant

Mowlam you're no fun gerry

Adams no fun – alright – i'll tell you something you already know but you can pretend you don't so it will seem like something new – trimble doesn't care what i think because he thinks i'm going to walk and this will all be sorted out without me in the room – and maybe i will walk – that hasn't been decided yet – it won't be sorted out without me though – and the bottom line is . . .

Blair (*to audience*) i like bottom lines – and the bottom line for gerry adams is – prisoners

Mowlam prisoners

Adams prisoners – we'll see how serious trimble is then – you can tell him that if you want

Mowlam he doesn't talk to me

Adams me neither

There are some Easter Lily badges on Adams table. Mowlam lifts one.

Mowlam nice badge – what is it

Adams an easter lily

Mowlam might wear one – does it suit me

Adams yes – probably keep in in your purse though – trimble would burst into flames if he saw you wearing that

Mowlam republican

Adams it's to remember the irish republican combatants who died or were executed after the 1916 easter rising against british rule in ireland

Mowlam right – better not then

They laugh.

Ahern is at his mother's funeral. Blair is in his office. Blair stands up and shouts at Ahern.

Blair it's all about strand two bertie – strand two

Ahern puts his hand up to acknowledge Blair. Blair sits down and Ahern continues with the funeral.

Hume meets Mowlam in a corridor.

Hume i hear trimble blew a fuse on the cross border bodies

Mowlam he's not happy

Hume	we want to move on strand one – (*To audience.*) strand one – a democratically elected assembly in northern ireland which is inclusive in its membership and subject to safeguards to protect the rights and interests of all sides of the community – and will be the prime source of authority in respect of all devolved responsibilities – i can't be any clearer than that

They all laugh.

back to mo

He returns to Mowlam.

Mowlam	he wants strand two sorted before he moves on anything
Hume	don't cave
Mowlam	i'm not
Hume	there's willing to talk and there's willing to talk – we're willing to talk – but – we're not willing to talk
Mowlam	(*to audience*) i'll pretend i understand that – maybe i've been here too long because in a way i sort of do understand it – (*To Hume.*) right – we're just talking about numbers – there's too many so they want a few less
Hume	it's nothing to do with numbers – (*To audience.*) it is a bit about numbers – (*To Mowlam.*) it's to see how far they can push bertie – tony has to rein trimble in – you talk to them
Mowlam	who listens to tea ladies
Hume	people needing tea for a start
Mowlam	if only

Adams shouts to Hume.

Adams   have you spoken to trimble yet

Hume   not really – he's under pressure

Adams   we all are

Blair shouts to Ahern.

Blair   bertie bertie

Ahern ignores him. Blair shouts towards Mowlam.

fuck fuck fuck

Mowlam enters.

fuck fuck fuck

Mowlam   tony calm down

Blair   no – fuck fuck fuck – we're not moving quickly enough

Mowlam   i've been here for months believe me this is quick

Blair   what's the point in me being here if nothing is happening

Mowlam   they're reading the document

Blair   reading the document – reading the fucking document – fuck the document – (*To audience.*) i don't mean that – documents are very important

Mowlam   detail is important in this place – every paragraph – every line – every word – every look – it all means something – that takes time

Blair   fuck time

Mowlam   do you want some tea

Blair   fuck tea – when is bertie back

Mowlam   this afternoon

Blair   fuck bertie – what's trimble doing

Mowlam	going through the document
Blair	fuck trimble – adams
Mowlam	the same
Blair	fuck adams – hume
Mowlam	(*to audience*) do you see a pattern developing – tony
Blair	i need to fucking talk to someone – mitchell – he knows everything – i'll get clinton on the phone
Mowlam	do you want me to tell you what i think
Blair	yes of course – how are you by the way – how is this all . . .

He points to her wig.

Mowlam	i'm fine
Blair	tired
Mowlam	yes but i'm fine
Blair	do you need some rest – maybe you should . . .
Mowlam	tony i'm fine – the important thing at the moment is to get trimble and ahern talking and then trimble and hume can start sorting out detail – i get the sense adams isn't going to move much until we get closer to the deadline
Blair	adams is vital
Mowlam	he'll take his time – at the moment if trimble isn't going to talk to him we have to do our best to move on – move on – and wait – we already know what it's going to be about anyway – prisoners
Blair	i know – i need to push trimble – i understand why he thinks the irish pushed their luck on strand two and cross border institutions but he

	has to move on strand one – maybe get mitchell to talk to him
Mowlam	you push it as well
Blair	what about decommissioning
Mowlam	there's no point in even thinking about that yet – that has to be after we've sorted out strands one and two
Blair	three years – we can get away with three years
Mowlam	he'll want less than that
Blair	he'll want one
Mowlam	two
Blair	unofficially maybe – stick with three though
Mowlam	yeah
Blair	talk to him maybe
Mowlam	i know what he's going to say – he has a mandate and he won't be ignored
Blair	i'll talk to mitchell and see if he'll talk to trimble
Mowlam	one of the protestant paramilitaries asked me because of the expected release of prisoners in a few years if he shot trimble now would he be out in two years
Blair	negotiable
Mowlam	i told him yes
	They laugh.
	i'll go and see adams
	Mowlam walks towards Adams. Mitchell is with Adams. Blair paces.
Mitchell	it would help things if you let it be known you're not going to walk

Adams	trimble is expecting me to walk
Mitchell	and will you
Adams	george
Mitchell	it's my job to ask these things gerry
Adams	what's happening with strand two
Mitchell	your input is required
Adams	we're thinking
Mitchell	in my experience too much thinking isn't always helpful gerry
Adams	neither is not enough george – talk to trimble
Mitchell	i'm talking to you
Adams	unionism has to move – talk to trimble
Mitchell	all involved have to move – there is no other option other than moving forward
Adams	who has held power in the north of ireland since its creation – trimble has to move – he has to understand that this can no longer be a unionist state – it's over
Mitchell	i think he knows that
Adams	knowing it and accepting it are two different things – he thinks this is the end and it's only really the start – you need to tell him that george – you can't sit on the fence here
Mitchell	i know what my job is
Adams	we all know what our jobs are – getting them done is another matter

Mitchell moves to Trimble's table. Trimble is doing some stretching exercises. Mowlam moves to Adams's table. Hume watches all this.

Mitchell	how are you
Trimble	back problems – you're like a bobbie on the beat
Mitchell	a bobbie on the beat
Trimble	(*to audience*) it grates me that america is involved in our business – it makes me feel like we can't look after our own affairs – that we can't be trusted – this is our place we'll deal with it – it complicates the situation – i'm more of a straightforward individual – that's how i see politics – choose a path and follow it – that's how i see life – but – it is what it is – and i'll deal with it – (*To Mitchell.*) a policeman patrolling his area
Mitchell	hardly a policeman
Trimble	a headmaster then
Mitchell	a referee
Trimble	yes a referee – (*He glances at the audience and smiles.*) strand two
Mitchell	i know – is there any point in asking about you talking to adams
Trimble	no – i'm offended that you even think you could ask
Mitchell	i must try every possible avenue
Trimble	if i had a gun pointed at your head would you be inclined to talk to me freely – would i be inclined to believe anything you said
	Mitchell moves to Hume's table. Trimble continues with his stretches.
Hume	what did the others have to say
Mitchell	prisoners – strand two – and then of course there was – prisoners – strand two

Trimble	(*to audience; stretching*) strand two – north south ministerial council – that is – north south bodies that could implement practical cooperation between northern ireland and southern ireland – agriculture education health and the like – interference in our affairs some would say
Hume	you know what's happening
Mitchell	does anyone
Hume	trimble gets articles two and three removed from the irish constitution and then limits the amount of cross border bodies in strand two and then shuts up shop – that's been his gameplan from the start
Mitchell	he knows he has to make a deal
Hume	what does the president think
Mitchell	i haven't had a chance to talk with him
Hume	what does he think
Mitchell	he will do whatever he can to make this work
Hume	and what do you tell him
Mitchell	that's between me and him
Hume	this has to work – it is the only way forward – (*To audience.*) this is the only way forward – the only game in town – trimble thinks adams wants to move too far and adams thinks trimble doesn't want to move at all – and me in the background dancing between the shadows – there are arguments to be had – what type of assembly – how many seats in said assembly – what type and how many cross border institutions – and then of course prisoners and guns – yet there is only one thing – get the deal done – get government up and running and then see where we go – that is the only way forward – the only way forward –

	i can't stress that enough – two traditions on a shared piece of rock – get the deal done and start moving forward – that's what i'm doing all the time – in the background – moving forward inch by inch – sometimes unnoticed – but that's ok – it's all about the big picture – (*To Mitchell.*) the only way forward
Mitchell	i'm here now – and i've been here a long time – i understand the situation john
Hume	we all appreciate the effort and time you have put into this george – this is the last hurdle – trimble has to understand what this is – unionist dominance is over – it's time to talk – time to negotiate a shared future

Mitchell moves to Blair. Mowlam is sitting with Adams. Trimble and Hume sit alone.

Adams	don't ask me if i want any tea
Mowlam	i wasn't going to
Adams	have you walked round the grounds
Mowlam	i've been meaning to but no
Adams	it's beautiful – saw a family of squirrels going about their daily business
Mowlam	did you disturb them
Adams	no – just watched
Mowlam	is that what you're doing now
Adams	this thing with trimble isn't just about guns – you understand
Mowlam	if you don't have a gun and are talking to a person with a gun it's a bit disconcerting
Adams	you have guns
Mowlam	it's not the same thing

Adams   it is to me and to the people i represent

Mowlam   is that it – is that what this boils down to

Adams   no – this is about equality – rights – citizens –
british unionist rule is over

Mowlam   you don't need a gun to gain equality – which you
have by the way so don't give me any of that shit

Adams   you don't live here you don't know

Mowlam   i've spoken to enough people to know what the
situation is – the thinking behind it all

Adams   you look after your end of things and i'll look
after mine – trimble needs to understand he's in
negotiations – tell him to stop issuing decrees
from on high

*Adams stretches out on the floor and goes to
sleep. Trimble shouts in Blair's direction.*

Trimble   she's too friendly with him

Mowlam   (*under her breath*) just doing my job

Blair moves to Trimble.

Blair   what would you have her do

Trimble   it isn't my place to tell her what to do

Blair   what would you have her do

Trimble   think about whose side she is on

Blair   i understand that you want to deal with me
directly that doesn't mean that i agree with your
assessment regarding my secretary of state for
northern ireland – she knows what she's doing –
you would do well to remember that – (*Moving
towards his desk. To audience.*) no yes prime
minister there

Trimble	(*to audience*) yes prime minister
	Mitchell and Blair at his desk.
Mitchell	i think trimble is right – strand two was too much too quick
Hume	(*to audience*) is there any need to explain strand two again – you all get it don't you – and if you haven't – pay attention
Blair	what is it i'm missing
Mitchell	missing
Blair	i'm missing something – there's a part of this situation i'm not getting – this should be more straightforward than it is
Mitchell	it's the way of things here
Blair	we need trimble and ahern to talk
	Ahern arrives. Papers are blown everywhere. He sits on his chair and gathers himself. As is always the case when he arrives everyone has to gather their papers up.
Mitchell	we need trimble and adams to talk
	They laugh.
Blair	where are we with everything
Mitchell	we need ahern and trimble to talk
	Trimble moves to Ahern's desk and sits.
Ahern	david
Trimble	bertie
Blair	(*to audience*) this is important – this is the foundation upon which we can move forward – this meeting of minds – of political beliefs – of national . . .

Mitchell indicates to him to tone it down a bit.
Blair gives him the thumbs up.

(*Whispers to Ahern and Trimble.*) go for it – keep her lit

Trimble and Ahern as before.

Trimble	it must be difficult times for you
Ahern	there's been easier days
Trimble	death is the hardest damn thing
Ahern	it is – i had to leave the funeral early
Trimble	politics can get in the way of everything

Silence.

Adams (*to audience*) it can be difficult – all those years of mistrust – the rumours – the violence – the silence – the blame game – the anger – the hatred – and yet we all walk the same path – all live within touching distance of each other – surrounded by the same water – divided by the same fields – we all know the same thing – that talking isn't always easy – but then what else have we got – cheek by jowl all of us – but as i say it can be difficult – you only need to listen to all this to know that

They shift in their seats.

Ahern we need to negotiate – there are no other options left

Trimble i can see that – we are under a time constraint

Ahern it is becoming increasingly difficult to discuss aspects of the agreement in isolation – and this is solely because of time and nothing else

Trimble solely because of time

Ahern	maybe we should look at . . .
Trimble	strands one and two . . .
Ahern	together rather than . . .
Trimble	concentrate on strand . . .
Ahern	two . . .
Trimble	alone
Ahern	ok – i have to get back to dublin – we can draw up papers and . . .
Trimble	yes draw up papers

Ahern exits. Helicopter blades, etc. Papers blown everywhere and as usual everyone gathers them up.

Blair looks up at the sky.

Blair	fuck fuck fuck
Mitchell	(*to audience*) and there we have it – fuck fuck fuck – another day brought to a close – (*To others.*) this is the last time anyone can adjourn until the talks are over one way or another
Trimble	(*to audience*) signs of movement in a stationary way
Hume	(*to audience*) positive discussions
Adams	(*to audience*) stuck
Mitchell	(*to audience*) and finally the tea lady
Mowlam	(*to audience*) where there's tea there's hope
Mitchell	(*to audience*) wise words indeed – and now back to the weather – it's going to get cold and snowy with maybe – maybe – a bit of light and heat – thursday the ninth of april – holy thursday – everything has to be done and dusted by midnight – if this were a dance – which it is – the hall's booked to midnight – so this is what you

might call – last dance thursday – just before this
all kicks off i feel i have to mention strand three

*Mock panic. The following lines are spoken over
each other.*

Blair   strand three – i don't know – what is that – did
            you know about this

Ahern   i thought i heard someone mention it but
            i thought it was a joke

Trimble   it's no joke – strand three

Adams   strand three – whatever – it isn't . . .

Hume   is it to do with . . . no it couldn't be that

Mitchell   (*to audience*) strand three covers east west
            relations between . . .

Hume   east west relations yeah that's it

Trimble   this is not about the republic gaining a say in the
            affairs of northern ireland this is a recalibration
            of relations between all parts of the british isles –
            this is not a joke

            *No one is interested. Mitchell goes to continue
            but Hume stops him and takes over.*

Hume   (*to audience*) . . . relations between london dublin
            belfast and other components of the united
            kingdom – scotland wales and the various self-
            governing islands – strand three

            *Ahern's helicopter lands – the usual – paper
            blown everywhere, etc. Ahern enters like he is late
            for class. He exchanges a look with Blair and
            takes his coat. Mowlam scans them all as if to
            say – 'are we all settled now'.*

Mitchell   (*to audience*) at some time during the day this did
            happen

33

*Trimble is at the urinals having a pee. Adams
enters he stands a few feet away and starts to pee.
There is an awkward silence. Adams looks at
Trimble. Trimble keeps his head down.*

Adams   is this where all the big lads hang out

*Trimble finishes peeing and zips his trousers up.
He passes Adams without looking at him.*

Trimble   grow up

*He exits. Adams finishes peeing and zips his
trousers up.*

Mitchell   (*to audience*) or might it have been better if this
happened

The same situation again.

Adams   is this where all the big lads hang out

As before.

Trimble   grow up

Adams   grow up – refusing to engage is that grown up –
david

Trimble   hand over your guns

Adams   that's not it – i know you say it is but it's not

Trimble   it is – i will not negotiate with anyone who has
a gun under the table

Adams   not anyone – republicans

Trimble   if you want me to admit i don't like you i have no
problem with that – i don't like you – or what
you stand for

Adams   you don't have to like what i stand for but you do
have to respect that i stand for it – that i represent
citizens who have beliefs and aspirations

Trimble   put the guns away

Adams	that's all you have isn't it
Trimble	no – i have democracy – i represent the majority
Adams	for the moment – we'll see what you're made of when that changes
Trimble	i am a democrat
Adams	so am i
Trimble	put the guns away
Adams	the guns are away – you just can't find them – a united ireland will either happen or it won't – this is about class – this is about sectarianism
Trimble	it's about killing – murder
Adams	war
Trimble	there was no war
Adams	what word would you use – or phrase – the troubles – oh look the troublesome irish are at it again – they're all drunk and they're burning their own houses down – how troublesome – the conflict
Trimble	it was needless
Adams	no it wasn't
Trimble	it would have . . .
Adams	it would've what – been alright if you all would've done what you were meant to – leave the running of this place to the people who know about those things – that's what this is all about isn't it – you just want to be left alone to run the place – to do the job you were born to do northern ireland a protestant state for a protestant people
Trimble	ok – when you look at me that's what you see – what do i see when i look at you

Adams   a second class citizen

Trimble   a terrorist – not a freedom fighter – not a
liberator – not a visionary – not a democrat –
a terrorist – that's who you are – that's how you
think – and you're so hurt – publicly hurt when
a person from the community you tried to destroy
says they don't trust you – your aim is to destroy
the thing i believe in – and no matter how many
times you say it isn't – i know it is – and that's
where we're at

*They take the positions they were in at the start of
the scene.*

Adams   is this where all the big lads hang out

As before.

Trimble   grow up

They both move back behind their chairs.

Radio   (*voice-over*) trevor deeney a thirty-four-year-old
former ulster volunteer force prisoner was shot
dead by the irish national liberation army in the
waterside area of derry

*The stage falls silent. They all stand alone. Adams
and Trimble exchange a look.*

Mowlam   (*to audience*) a reminder of the place we're in

Movement returns. Blair moves to Trimble.

Blair   david what is your assessment of the situation

Trimble   nothing much has changed prime minister – strand
two needs to be re-negotiated – it is too expansive –
dublin has too much of a say in our affairs

Blair   besides strand two where are we at

Trimble   strand one is negotiable – the rest is uncertain
because i imagine at some stage adams will walk

Adams (*to audience*) strand one – democratic institutions in the north of ireland . . .

Trimble (*to audience*) northern ireland

Adams (*to audience*) . . . that is – a devolved power sharing assembly between unionist and nationalist parties

Blair what are you saying

Trimble i can work with hume

Blair you think you can form some type of power sharing administration with hume – and leave adams and paisley shouting from the side lines

Trimble i can work with hume

Blair you don't see the need for these negotiations to be all inclusive

Trimble did you not hear me

Blair i heard

Trimble paisley wants to take over and you're better with me than him – and adams is the enemy – his end goal is to destroy northern ireland as a political entity – as a country – he wants to break up the – your – united kingdom – you need to wake up to that fact – everything he says or does is geared towards that objective

Blair don't lecture me i know who i'm dealing with – we both want an end to violence – as do many others – after that it is up to you the politicians of northern ireland to create a better society – northern ireland has stood still while the world moved on – this is your chance to catch up – i'll talk to bertie about strand two and i will relate your thoughts to him – because i am your prime minister don't think i will back you no matter what – we are here to negotiate – we are here to be reasonable

Trimble	you're talking to the reasonable one prime minister

Trimble exits to his chair. Blair rolls up a sheet of paper into a ball and throws it at Ahern. He keeps doing this until Ahern notices. He moves to Blair's chair.

Blair	trimble says . . .
Ahern	just stop right there –
Blair	i have to tell you what he says
Ahern	i know what he says – it's the same bloody thing time and again
Blair	this is about listening to the . . .
Ahern	alright – alright – what did he say
Adams	(*to audience*) what did trimble say – what did trimble say – we know what trimble said – we always know what trimble says – what did hume say – what did adams say – over and over again – this is the only thing i know about all of this – i know it has to play itself out – one way or another it has to play itself out

Pause.

Blair	what do you think he said
Ahern	oh fuck off

They laugh.

Blair	less cross border institutions and they have to be under the control of a northern ireland executive
Ahern	if they are controlled through the north whenever the unionists feel like it they'll just not bother with them – your problem is you trust the unionists too much

Blair	fuck the unionists – (*To audience.*) i didn't mean that forget i said it – (*To Ahern.*) all i'm trying to do is move forward
Ahern	well move forward by reining them in – i keep saying this and no one seems to get it . . .
Blair	i know – you're changing your constitution
Ahern	don't say it as if it's nothing
Blair	i'm not bertie but . . .
Ahern	but what
Blair	we have to move on
Ahern	i need something in return
Blair	peace
Ahern	don't pull that stunt – we all want that – get trimble to talk to hume about stage one at the same time we're talking about strand two – we need to know that he sees the bigger picture – trimble has to get it into his head that the north is still part of the island of ireland which means we have every right to be involved
Blair	get him moving on strand one – yes – take his mind off you foreigners
Ahern	we're in ireland boy – you're the foreigner
Blair	it feels like it – i'll get him to talk to hume

Ahern moves back to his desk. Blair coughs directly at Trimble. Trimble finishes his stretches and goes to Blair.

you have to talk to hume

Trimble	we are in the process of discussing . . .
Blair	not strand two strand one

Trimble	we will not . . .
Blair	listen – this rests on you at the moment so think clearly here – if you are seen to be engaging on strand one strand two will follow
Trimble	this just isn't me i have to bring others along – a few of my front line colleagues have already walked out
Blair	you knew that was going to happen
Trimble	yes
Blair	well then
Trimble	knowing it doesn't help – i need to be seen to be winning all the time
Blair	that isn't going to happen – we all knew that from the start
Trimble	what we all knew doesn't matter
Blair	yes it fucking does – i am your prime minister and i am advising you to do something
Trimble	i am well aware prime minister . . .
Blair	stop calling me that
Trimble	what
Blair	stop calling me prime minister
Trimble	i don't understand prime minister
Blair	it annoys me
Trimble	i'm sorry but you just called yourself prime minister prime minister
Blair	you use it and then ignore me as if i wasn't your prime minister – i am as your prime minister advising you to do something – talk to john hume about his strand one proposals

Trimble	i shall think about that prime minister and get back to you
Blair	don't think about it too long
Trimble	i have people to talk to tony
Blair	you do that david

Trimble moves back to his chair.

fuck it – don't like him calling me tony either – boss – (*Shouts over to Trimble.*) say i have people to talk to boss

Trimble	i have people to talk to boss
Blair	no that's not it – thanks anyway

Adams moves to Hume.

Adams	i'm being ignored
Hume	i told you i'll keep you posted
Adams	no – not enough
Hume	i'll be talking to trimble about strands one and two and i'll . . .
Adams	i don't want everything coming through you
Hume	talk to bertie then
Adams	nobody wants to talk about prisoners
Hume	all you want to talk about is prisoners
Adams	the situation hasn't changed – it's a mark of how serious people are regarding the negotiations – trimble would be happy if we walked
Hume	what's new – why are you here
Adams	because i represent . . .
Hume	because . . .

Adams	because i represent a significant proportion of the electorate
Hume	because i insisted that you are here – because i pointed out that if you weren't here i wouldn't be here – because we have moved on – because i have a vision of a new ireland within a new europe
Adams	and if i walk where does that leave you
Hume	is that it – is that your ultimate answer to everything – we'll walk
Adams	what would you do if we did
Hume	i don't see the point in . . .
Adams	what would you do
Hume	it is not up to me to . . .
Adams	what would you do – would you stay or go – would you continue to negotiate with trimble if we walked
Hume	negotiate – trimble wants to talk
Adams	mention prisoners – how's blair
Hume	he doesn't understand here
Adams	like every other british prime minister before him – do you trust him
Hume	he wants a solution
Adams	do you trust him
Hume	maybe – do you
Adams	maybe
Hume	paisley's outside
Adams	i heard that
Hume	it was only a matter of time

Adams	trimble must be looking over his shoulder
Hume	he never gives the impression that he thinks that
	They both laugh.
	paisley will be involved at some stage
Adams	people voted for him – have to listen to what he says
Hume	might have to share power with him
Adams	if that's the way of it that's the way of it – he wouldn't though
Hume	don't know about that – he wants to be king
	Hume moves back to his chair. He eyes Trimble who is doing back exercises.
	Mowlam moves to Blair.
Ahern	(*to audience*) to put this all in context there are other things happening in the world – we just don't know much about them – although i'm sure they know about us – maybe the way to think about that is – the world's looking at us and we are looking at each other
Mowlam	just saw hume and adams talking
Blair	i don't have a good feeling about any of this
Mowlam	why
Blair	beyond the obvious reasons of where we are and who the fuck we're dealing with
Mowlam	yes
Blair	i've been trying to get in contact with bertie and he's gone missing – he's planning something and adams and hume know about it – maybe
Mowlam	you have to assume that it's not all going to go your way

43

Blair   try telling trimble that – fucking nightmare

Mowlam   be positive

Blair   positive – fuck being positive

Mowlam   ahern is waiting on trimble and hume to meet – who both assume they will battle over strand two but will agree on strand one – because there is agreement on strand one they won't want to balls up strand two so there'll be a compromise – then it's just dotting i's and crossing t's

Blair   what about adams – prisoners – guns

Mowlam   adams says yes to everything

They laugh.

ahern and hume get adams to agree to three years for prisoner release and we work out some type of plan for decommissioning – which is really only an agreement not to use the guns as they're not going to hand them in anyway they're going to bury them – then – we all wait a few years and paisley gets tired shouting from the side lines and joins the ranks – then we have paisley and adams as first and deputy first minister – imagine a world where that would happen

They laugh again.

Blair   and if not that

Mowlam   if not that we're fucked

Blair   we're fucked then

Mowlam   i'm going to make some tea

Blair   if you see bertie . . .

Mowlam   tell him . . .

Blair   tell him – fuck – i don't know

Mowlam   ok i'll tell him that then

Mitchell   (*to audience*) i was told a joke the other day and it reminded me i wasn't from here – a man walks into a bakery and asks for a pan loaf – the baker says i don't have a pan but do you want a plain – the man says no thank you i've a bike outside

Adams, Trimble and Hume all laugh. Mitchell, Blair, Mowlam and Ahern don't laugh.

(*To audience.*) i don't get it – i just don't get it

Adams approaches Mitchell and signals to Blair, Mowlam and Ahern to come to him.

Adams   in ireland we have two types of loaves – bertie you should've got this

Ahern   i didn't

Adams   pan loaves and plain loaves – so – do you have a pan loaf – no but do you want a plain – you with me – a plain – the guy says – no thank you i have a bike outside

Trimble and Hume laugh.

Hume   a plane – a plane – an aircraft – jesus christ – it doesn't matter – how can you not get that

They all move back to their places.

Hume and Trimble meet in the middle of the stage.

Mowlam   (*to audience*) the unionists want an assembly – the nationalists want north south institutions – the unionists fear that the nationalists will work to make the north south institutions work and then scupper the assembly – the nationalists on the other hand fear that the unionists will work to make the assembly function and then scupper the north south institutions – the unionists want the assembly to be in control of the north south institutions while the nationalists want dublin and london to be in control of them – so just so we're all straight on this – strand two cross border institutions and strand one the assembly

Trimble a system of local authority based along the lines of the welsh model

Hume no

Trimble there would be executive committees

Hume but no ministers

Trimble executive committees that would take control of the day to day running of northern ireland

Hume answerable to who

Trimble we would always be answerable to westminister

Hume and you think that's acceptable

Trimble i think it's workable

Hume so basically back to the old stormont with you as king of the north but with probably less power than stormont had

Trimble i can't sit in government with adams

Hume i'm not being part of some backdoor unionist agenda – we both know what would happen – every time you had problems with an issue you'd run to westminister

Trimble as if you wouldn't run to dublin

Hume i want us all to be part of a traditional executive with proper ministers in charge of their own departments – we are not returning to the old stormont

Trimble   that's not what i'm suggesting – regarding allocations of chairmanships of local authorities we can use the d'hondt system

Mowlam   (*to audience*) no one really knows what the d'hondt system actually is – except d'hondt and a few others – for the purposes of this conversation we're talking about proportional representation with a few other bits and pieces – the point is you need the support of others to get something passed – cooperation is what we're talking about

Hume   no matter what we decide we can use d'hondt – why are we doing this – all this – these negotiations – hours days talking – paper after paper after paper – endless discussions – what

Trimble   i don't appreciate your tone

Hume   i don't appreciate the notion that you think you can get what you want and then say no to the rest – and don't tell me about the pressure you're under because . . .

Trimble   because what – because we're all under the same pressure – no we're not – what pressure are you under – where's the dissent in your ranks – maybe one or two shouting from the back of the room – you waltz around nipping in and out of meetings with nothing to say other than – let's all crack on – what is it you have to sell to your party – they're queuing up behind me . . .

Hume   shut up shut up shut up – jesus christ – move forward – move fucking forward

Silence.

Trimble   just understand the situation i'm in

Hume   i do – we need to trust each other

Trimble	we do
Hume	so
Trimble	so

Ahern coughs. Trimble takes a deep breath and gathers himself, then moves to Ahern.

Ahern	cross border institutions
Trimble	none
Ahern	ok – articles two and three of the irish constitution are off the table

Silence.

Ahern	will we start again
Trimble	ok
Ahern	do you agree in principle that there should be cross border institutions as part of this agreement
Trimble	no
Ahern	right

Silence.

Trimble	right
Ahern	right
Trimble	right
Ahern	right

Silence.

Trimble takes a deep breath.

Trimble	your list is too long – it runs to three pages for god's sake – i won't sell that – but even if i wanted to how could i – three pages – do you have any understanding of unionism whatsoever

Ahern	have you no understanding of articles two and three – we are changing our constitution – for once i would appreciate it if you unionists understood that – stopping treating that as if it was nothing and this is all some type of bartering fucking game – cross border institutions are happening – how many is negotiable – so negotiate

Trimble stands in silence.

Ahern	negotiate
Trimble	environment
Ahern	education
Trimble	i'll have to think about that
Ahern	it makes practical sense – tourism
Trimble	yes – transport
Ahern	waterways

Hume coughs.

Trimble goes back to Hume.

Trimble	alright
Hume	alright what
Trimble	the assembly
Hume	you're running with what i suggested
Trimble	yes – i have always been willing to compromise – i am getting what i want regarding strand two and the changes to the irish constitution – so – power sharing
Mowlam	(*to audience*) power sharing – one – either parallel consent – or – two – a weighted majority – either way a majority of unionists and nationalists must vote for a bill to get it through the chamber

Trimble	one other thing
Hume	what
Trimble	first minister and deputy first minister – those titles are written in stone
Hume	they are of equal power
Trimble	i understand that – but it is first minister and deputy first minister or nothing
Hume	or nothing
Trimble	i need it to sweeten the pill
Hume	i understand – first and deputy first minister it is

Trimble goes to his seat and uses it to stretch his back. Hume dances round the tables. He goes to Adams. He is in a buoyant mood.

trimble just agreed to strand one – it was all no no no – everything as before – and then – he agreed – he talked to bertie about strand two . . .

Adams	strand two
Hume	that was always going to be the case
Adams	that can only mean less cross border bodies
Hume	the number was always negotiable – what's left won't be nothing – bertie wouldn't let the whole thing . . .

Adams moves straight to Ahern. They stand in silence for a moment. Hume dances in between all the desks back to his own.

Adams	the rumour is you caved
Ahern	gerry hold on a minute i . . .
Adams	john just said to me you . . .
Ahern	nothing is finalised yet – we're still talking

Adams	i'm going to walk
Ahern	it's a negotiation
Adams	so you did or you didn't pull back on the cross border institutions
Ahern	trimble wants none i want plenty – we had to meet somewhere in the middle
Adams	unionism has to be weakened
Ahern	nothing's decided yet – he's getting what he wants with stage one i hear – so – i'll push on strand two
Adams	it looks like trimble is calling the shots
Ahern	he's not
Adams	everything's in his favour – setting up the assembly – articles two and three – all this nonsense too about first minister and deputy first minister – this was meant to be about releasing prisoners not the coronation of a king
Ahern	strand two isn't negotiated yet – he's jumped the gun
Adams	you have to pull back
Ahern	or
	Silence.
Ahern	i'll do what i think is the right thing for the country that i lead
Adams	we all have to do what we think is the right thing
Ahern	you represent a party i represent a country
	Silence.
Adams	maybe all this is too soon
Ahern	or the best chance that you have

Adams	we'll see
Ahern	blair wants this done
Adams	and what
Ahern	that's not nothing – he mightn't know everything about the situation here but . . .
Adams	don't tell me he's the right person for the job
Ahern	he's the right person for the job
Adams	he looks after his own interests
Ahern	his head's in the future
Adams	his head's up his arse

They laugh.

Ahern	i'll talk to him – make sure he's not just listening to trimble – are you going to walk
Adams	i'll do what i always do
Ahern	and what's that
Adams	the right thing

Ahern and Adams go back to their seats. Blair throws a ball of paper at Trimble (he keeps doing this until he hits him). Trimble stands, stretches a few times, and then moves to Blair.

Blair	what's the situation
Trimble	it isn't all sorted yet prime minister but we're moving in the right direction
Blair	you spoke with bertie
Trimble	yes
Blair	and strand two is – what
Trimble	ongoing – and strand one is sorted – i just have to sell it to my party

Hume	(*to audience*) last time – strand one – democratic institutions – that is – devolved power sharing assembly between unionist and nationalist parties – strand two – north south (*He smiles at Adams.*) ministerial council – that is – north south bodies that could implement practical cooperation between northern ireland and ireland
Blair	do you envisage problems
Trimble	yes of course – i have to sell it
Blair	what is your feeling about it
Trimble	i try not to have feelings about anything
Blair	gut instinct then
Trimble	if i have the senior members of the party with me that should be enough but it'll be close – i keep trying to explain this to you – there is a lot of mistrust and ill feeling towards nationalism stroke republicanism – that doesn't go away easily
Blair	but you will push the document
Trimble	why do you think i'm here
Blair	yes – of course
Hume	(*to audience*) there is other stuff happening in the world at the moment but if we're going to be honest about it this is the only game in town – and on the more disruptive side of things paisley is starting to make some noise – i don't know what the weather report is because i haven't looked out of the window in two days

Ahern bumps into Mowlam in a corridor.

Mowlam	i'm very sorry about your mother
Ahern	thank you – over this last week i've passed her house on the way to meetings – i could've called in – i should've called in

Mowlam	i'm sure she knew the importance of what you're doing
Ahern	that doesn't change anything – damn thing takes over your whole bloody life – every waking hour
Mowlam	at the moment i'm glad of that
Ahern	sorry
Mowlam	no need to be
Ahern	how are you
Mowlam	tired – thinking about death a lot – sorry
Ahern	no – same here
Mowlam	not in a morbid way
Ahern	no of course not
Mowlam	it's hard to shift
Ahern	i know – still have to get on with it though
Mowlam	that's all there is – just getting on with it – so – where are we on things
Ahern	i'm on my way to see tony about . . .
Mowlam	talk to me first
Ahern	i don't think . . .
Mowlam	i have a better understanding of the situation than he does
Ahern	ok – i met with trimble and we had an open and honest discussion on the scope and depth of strand two
Mowlam	the amount of cross border institutions
Ahern	on reflection . . .
Mowlam	don't tell me you . . .

Ahern	on reflection i decided that the original number of cross border institutions was the one we were going with
Mowlam	it's too many – you know it's too many
Ahern	it's what i'm going with
Mowlam	we've spent all this fucking time trying to get trimble on fucking board and now this – you know this is a fucking deal breaker – you know he'll walk
Ahern	he's always threatening to walk
Mowlam	why risk it
Ahern	why risk it – why fucking risk it – this is ireland – this is my country
Mowlam	this is british soil
Ahern	fuck british soil – do you think for one minute i'm going to let some uppity fucking unionist dictate my country's involvement in this
Mowlam	that's it – that's how you're going to fucking deal with this – what happened – i bet i know what happened – gerry came running to you crying that those bad unionists are getting everything – and it's so fucking dreadful – what did you think was going to happen – fucking grow up
Ahern	this is it isn't it – no matter what the fuck is ever said it boils down to the english being the only adults in the room – listen to me . . .
Mowlam	don't talk to me like that
Ahern	i'll talk to you whatever the fuck way i want – you'll be long gone and this will still . . .
Mowlam	fuck you
Ahern	i didn't mean – no no no no – i meant . . .

Mowlam   i know what you meant

Ahern   mo listen to me – i meant your administration – please don't think – i wouldn't ever – i – i – i wouldn't . . .

Mowlam   it's ok – really – i know

Silence.

there's still too many cross border bodies

Ahern   talk to trimble – sorry get tony to talk to trimble – how are you by the way

Mowlam   as if you cared

Ahern   . . .

Mowlam   i'm joking – tired – i'll have to go on the drip for a while

Ahern   i could do with going on that myself

Mowlam   just the rest of the day to go

Ahern   no pressure

The noise of the gathered media – cameras flashing, etc. Adams is giving a press conference.

Adams   i don't know exactly what is being said and who is saying it – although i have a fair idea – i am here now to tell you that at this moment in time there is no agreement – and as far as sinn fein are concerned it looks unlikely there will be an agreement – that does not mean to say that effort isn't being made – it is – but sometimes with all the will in the world things just don't work out – that does not mean there won't be other opportunities – there will always be other opportunities – thank you

The Press   (*voice-over*) gerry – gerry – gerry – gerry – gerry

Adams returns to his seat.

Trimble bursts into Blair's office.

Trimble   i just listened to adams and i've heard the rumours coming out of ahern's office – there will be no agreement based on the current strand two proposals – i could not have made myself clearer about this prime minister – strand two is unacceptable

Blair   david i will handle it

Trimble   that press conference makes it look like adams is in control of everything – the idea that it didn't suit him this time but he may come back to it – i have tried to explain this to you several times how difficult this is for me – this isn't helping – you need to talk to . . .

Blair   i'll talk it through with . . .

Trimble   the irish government

Blair   bertie

Trimble   whoever

Trimble returns to his seat.

Blair and Ahern meet centre stage.

Silence.

Ahern   i'm under pressure tony from all sides – and don't tell me a damn thing about trimble i don't want to hear

Blair   i thought this was settled

Ahern   what is it we're trying to do

Blair   herd sheep

Ahern   specifically – right now

Blair	same answer
Ahern	adams won't walk
Blair	how do you know
Ahern	there's no advantage to it
Blair	trimble
Ahern	i don't trust him – i can't get rid of that thought – strand two is what we gain – take control of that – put him in his place
Blair	i know – he's tricky
Ahern	he respects you
Blair	does he
Ahern	no

They laugh.

he respects the job

Blair	you and i agree now – we need to be in control
Ahern	a press release
Blair	yes
Ahern	ok – we move forward together now until it's over
Blair	right
Ahern	right

Blair and Ahern stand together in the middle of the stage.

Blair	we have come to an agreement
Ahern	an agreement – we shall move forward together
Blair	move forward together

Flashing cameras. The two men acknowledge the attention.

Hume   (*to audience*) the negotiations are progressing at a steady pace – progress has been made on strand two which has in turn allowed for progress to be made on strand one – talks are ongoing and we are slowly moving towards our midnight deadline

The two men go back to their chairs. Mowlam moves to Blair.

Adams   (*to audience*) between one and two a.m. – i had a talk with the protestant paramilitaries about the possibility of a united front on prisoner release

He moves his head from side to side as if in conversation, then stands back as if being shouted at.

that could've gone better

Blair   who said thursday was the deadline

Mowlam   you

Blair   me

Mowlam   family holiday in spain with prime minister Aznar – (*To audience.*) it's well for some

Blair   i do like deadlines – clear – precise – focused

Mowlam   have you to go back to london before you meet up with the family

Blair   hadn't thought about that

Mowlam   need a toothbrush

Blair   indeed

Adams enters.

Adams   saw the light on

Mowlam   there's a joke about that

Adams   a moth

Mowlam	yeah
Blair	have you a response to the draft paper
Adams	which draft paper
Blair	the last one
Adams	no
Mowlam	gerry . . .
Adams	you know the procedure – i just wanted to call in – and – look don't be too disappointed if it doesn't work out this time around
Mowlam	why is there something . . .
Adams	i'm just saying – people seem to be caught up on certain things – and i'm just saying maybe . . .
Blair	strand two – strand two is . . .
Adams	it's not just that – there are other things that maybe . . .
Mowlam	maybe what
Adams	maybe aren't being given due consideration
Blair	are you going to walk
Adams	i didn't say that – i could – but i didn't say that
Mowlam	you're all the bloody same do you know that – the same every fucking time – it's this – no it mightn't be this – if it was this then it would have to be this – and if they have we need to have – say what it fucking is gerry
Adams	it's not just one thing i'm talking about . . .
Blair	three years – the british public will not understand letting out ira terrorists
Adams	a year – they are political prisoners and their release is crucial to this process

Mowlam	we can't do a year – we just can't do it – there would be uproar
Adams	it's a sign of your commitment
Blair	i'm here – that's the only sign you need
Adams	a year
Mowlam	no – three years
Adams	i was just popping in – these things can be discussed anytime
Blair	two
Mowlam	tony
Blair	two
Adams	can you commit to that
Blair	no
Adams	i have your word
Blair	you have my word i'll try
Adams	we'll leave it at that
Mowlam	you can't mention this
Adams	i know – so the dentist says to the moth – what you need is a psychiatrist i'm a dentist – and the moth says i know but i just saw the light on

Adams goes back to his seat.

Blair	what do you think
Mowlam	the truth
Blair	of course the fucking truth
Mowlam	neither of us will like it
Blair	what's new
Mowlam	eventually we're going to have to say one year – it mightn't happen but we're going to have to say it

Blair	in private
Mowlam	of course in private
Blair	a last resort
Mowlam	a last resort
Blair	you say it – easier denied if you say it
Mitchell	(*to audience*) so – where are we – this is the problem – nobody knows where we are at any one time – everyone knows where they are but no one knows where everyone is – hume is happy things are moving forward – trimble is happy things are standing still – ahern happyish in that him and tony are seeing eye to eye – blair – that's tricky – he's a bundle of something – a bundle of what though – adams – well we see in a minute – and mo – well she's just doing her job

He hands Mowlem a document. She quickly flicks through it and moves to Adams. A full-on shouting match.

Mowlam	are you fucking kidding me – forty pages – forty fucking pages – now – what the fuck are we meant to do with this – there's no time to go through all of this
Adams	so you've read it then
Mowlam	fuck off
Adams	you asked for a response to your draft document
Mowlam	this is disruptive – fuck you gerry
Adams	you asked sinn fein for a response to your draft document and this is it
Mowlam	it's your exit strategy that's what it is
Adams	it is our response to . . .

Mowlam stop it – just stop it

Silence.

Adams prisoners released in one year

Mowlam you know what tony said

Adams never mind tony

Mowlam two years

Adams no

Mowlam the unionists will walk

Adams i don't care – say it

Mowlam two years

Adams no

Mowlam two years – and what about decommissioning

Adams it is what it is

Mowlam say it

Adams it will happen

Mowlam when

Adams say it

Mowlam prisoner release in one year if we can

Adams decommissioning will be orderly and practical

Mowlam and total

Adams and total – are we agreed

Mowlam we are agreed

Hume and Ahern bump into each other in the corridor. They are both on their way to meetings.

Hume trimble

Ahern blair

Hume	stage two
Ahern	the irish language – as he would call it
Hume	how you fairing
Ahern	alright – it'll hit me when this is all over
Hume	it will
Ahern	you getting any sleep
Hume	no – you
Ahern	no
Hume	half the time you're thinking about the future of the country and the other half you're thinking of bed
Ahern	sleep for a week after this – there's nothing we need to talk about at the moment is there
Hume	don't think so – i'll let you know how it goes with him
Ahern	aye – do you want me to keep you posted on the ulster scots end of things
Hume	no
Ahern	if there's other stuff comes up i'll let you know
Hume	right
Ahern	right

They move on.

A clock strikes midnight. They all look at each other, shake their heads, and then look away.

Mitchell (*to audience*) the deadline passes – the reverend ian paisley – a man once listened to and followed by tens of thousands of loyalists – arrives on the scene to gloat at the failure of the talks with no

more than a few hundred supporters demanding
to be heard – when no one of any real worth
came out to play the reverend was taken aback –
how could they talk to terrorists and murderers
and at least one homosexual and not to him –
he found a tent and held a press conference

Everyone on stage – watches the television.

Newsreader   (*voice-over*) the room packed to the rafters –
trimble is a traitor and these talks are an act of
treachery – and then – from the back of the hall –
from loyalists who once thought the reverend
ian's every word gospel came

Crowd   (*voice-over; chanting*)
oh the grand old duke of york
he had ten thousand men
he marched them up to the top of the hill
and he marched them down again
and when they were up they were up
and when they were down they were down
and when they were only halfway up
they were neither up nor down

Newsreader   (*voice-over*) there was another time when all
that would've mattered more than it does now –
a government spokesperson with long experience
in northern ireland said – once he would've
brought thousands – tens of thousands with him –
now a few hundred – look at those loyalists many
of them once thought him a god – they went out
and killed thinking he was saving the union –
now they've turned on him – it is the end of an
era – time moves on without favour or mercy –
and now the weather – howling winds coupled
with bouts of driving rain – you couldn't make
this stuff up – well you could and people often
do – back to the talks – and one last thing – the

65

views expressed in this broadcast are not mine
nor that of the good people i work for – that's all
i'm saying – don't shoot the messenger

They all turn their televisions off.

A ticking clock in the background.

Mowlam friday the tenth of april – good friday – all the
caterers have gone home – not a bite to be had

Mitchell to Blair.

Mitchell this is the last day . . .

Mitchell to Ahern.

no matter what happens we're . . .

Mitchell to Mowlam.

leaving here – either we have something or we don't

Mowlam adams isn't playing ball – we have to concentrate
on hume and trimble – that's what's going to get
us over the line

Mitchell we can't leave anyone behind

Mowlam how is that thought helpful

Mitchell it's the reality of our situation

Mowlam and what

Mitchell it needs to be pointed out

Mowlam no it doesn't – every dog in the street knows
that – the situation is we can only do what we can
only do

Mitchell i know that

Mowlam say this doesn't happen

Mitchell i know

Mowlam you know what

Mitchell	i know the importance of that
Mowlam	if this doesn't happen now it needs to end in a way that allows it to happen further down the road – the only way that happens is for everyone to be given an opportunity to say – we tried
Mitchell	we are trying – if it doesn't happen now it may not happen until when
Mowlam	again – and what
Mitchell	i'm just saying – i don't know what i'm saying – i can't think straight – i'm exhausted
Mowlam	me too – adams will do something – i know him – he won't just walk away – none of them will – it may not happen but no one's walking away
Mitchell	we'll see
Mowlam	i was talking to the loyalists about prisoner release – they have their doubts about trimble – they think he's both weak and a glory hunter
Mitchell	he's trying

Hume and Trimble. Hume is pacing. Trimble is stretching.

Trimble	i'm a democrat
Hume	we'll all democrats
Trimble	no we're not – we don't all have arms dumps hidden all over the country
Hume	david this issue . . .
Trimble	this issue what john
Hume	you can't get hung up on it
Trimble	that doesn't mean it should be ignored
Hume	jesus christ – how is it being ignored

Trimble it feels like everyone is hoping i'll forget about it – it'll just slip by unnoticed

Hume i'm lost for words – you make decommissioning a major issue . . .

Trimble how is getting rid of guns in society not a major issue

Hume you know what i mean

Trimble but you don't know what i mean – if they're there they're still a threat – and what's more to the point they're a reminder that they were used

Hume you make this a major issue yet you refuse to talk to the people who have the guns – don't – i know – i know – i don't want to get into this again

Trimble it won't go away

Hume i know – let's move on

Trimble (*to audience*) let's move on – i don't believe it is the same for us all – i am trying my best to move on – to move forward – in fact i think we all are although i take no pride in saying that – i know all the arguments so there is no point in looking at me and saying there is another point of view – i know that – in the same way i know who votes for me and why they vote for me – this has to do with me – my head is full of the law – that's difficult to shift – there's right and there's wrong – (*To Hume.*) ok

Hume right – an elected assembly

Trimble yes – right – elected members from all parties but – i can't be seen to be working with sinn fein in government

Hume surely that depends on . . .

Trimble in principle

Hume	you can't enter into an election and then say you won't work with one of the parties elected
Trimble	ok – say i say everything is ok – if needs be we'll sit in government with sinn fein – and they haven't handed over a single gun or ounce of explosives – and if they refuse to all i can do is walk out and be blamed for bringing the whole thing down – what i'm suggesting is . . .
Hume	it's not going to work
Trimble	what i'm suggesting is . . .
Hume	there has to be a cross community coalition
Trimble	let me finish john – have an election – form a government and when the ira have decommissioned sinn fein can take their place according to their vote percentage
Hume	and you think that's acceptable to them
Trimble	i'm suggesting it be acceptable to us
Hume	well it isn't – what i am suggesting is a cross community . . .
Trimble	coalition chosen government in which all the parties work together to make decisions – and it's ok if somebody has a gun under the table – and at the same time by the way we'll release all the prisoners – look this is getting us nowhere
Hume	let's park decommissioning and prisoners
Trimble	right
Hume	right – we allocate government jobs to each party on their electoral strength . . .
Trimble	but only a few decisions – for example . . .
Hume	the budget

Trimble	the budget – requires formal cross community agreement
Hume	which would require all parties to be involved – right
Trimble	we have to think it through
Hume	i know – i know – but as a starting point
Trimble	as a starting point – maybe
Mowlam	(*to audience*) as a starting point – as always happens with these types of things the nearer you get to the end the more chance there is of it all kicking off – alastair campbell – the government's press guru – on getting word of the trimble hume meeting tells the press that an agreement is very close – which was of course jumping the gun – so to speak
	(*to audience*) ten past one
	Blair has no tie on and his shirtsleeves rolled up. Trimble is dressed as neatly as he always is.
Trimble	ninety elected representatives prime minister
Blair	ninety
Trimble	the assembly has to be of a manageable size
Blair	manageable size – that sounds like . . .
Trimble	any administration has to be a manageable size
Blair	right – there's flexibility though
Trimble	i am nothing if not flexible prime minister
Hume	(*to audience*) one forty-five a.m.
Ahern	there has to be . . .
Blair	there will be . . .
Ahern	i know but . . .

Blair	but nothing . . .
Ahern	what about . . .
Blair	i'm dealing with . . .
Ahern	what am i talking about
	Silence.
Blair	the irish language
	They laugh.
Ahern	you guessed that didn't you
Blair	i'm good
Ahern	the irish language
Blair	they're going to push back on this
Ahern	it's important – it's fundamental – how can there be a logic to cross border institutions if there isn't an acceptance of the irish language
Blair	did you use the word logic
	They laugh.
Ahern	i'm exhausted
Blair	i know
Ahern	you can't let the unionists sweep aside the notion of the irish language – it's a . . .
Blair	i know what it is
Trimble	(*to audience*) two a.m. – blair was meant to be on holiday with his family at spanish prime minister aznar's official residence in the south of spain – and maybe just for a split second he is
	Blair relaxes in his chair as if sunbathing. He takes a sip of a long cool drink. He gets out of the chair and dives into the sea. He swims around all the desks. He arrives back at his chair and sits down.

Adams (*to audience*) two fifteen – blair has stopped swimming and we're back to work on dry land

Blair right – right – so – me and then all of this – strand one hume and trimble – strand two trimble and hume – arms trimble and adams – prisoner release adams and trimble – irish language adams – ulster scots – scotch – scots – scotch – scots scots – irish constitution – i'm missing something – fuck – fuck – something to do with – something to do with island – your island – my island – these islands – strand three – keep forgetting about that – must get someone to explain it to me – right start again – strand one hume and trimble – strand two (*To audience.*) sometimes you forget what you've said and who you've said it to – if trimble knew i said to adams prisoner release might be a year – it's not worth thinking about – fucking minefield

Hume sighs and shakes his head. Blair shakes his head and sighs.

Mowlam (*to audience*) two thirty a.m. mitchell and president clinton on the phone

She coughs and clears her throat.

Clinton (*voice-over*) what's the situation george – are we close to a deal

Mitchell this is northern ireland mister president

Clinton laughs.

Clinton (*voice-over*) is progress being made

Mitchell yes and no

Clinton (*voice-over*) i'll just keep phoning and talking then

Mitchell yes mister president – the way i would describe the present situation is low level panic – it looks like a deal might happen so they panic a bit and

start introducing shit that doesn't really matter –
then the shit that doesn't really matter turns into
something that does matter – so we move back
a few steps and reassure everyone – and this leads
us back to the shit that doesn't matter

Clinton (*voice-over*) it sounds like you have that shit
under control george

They laugh.

Mitchell the next few hours will be important

Clinton (*voice-over*) if i can help in any way just let me
know

Mitchell of course mister president – i can assure you that
everyone appreciates your involvement

Clinton (*voice-over*) it's ireland george – i'm the president
of the united states of america – how could i not
be involved

Mitchell yes mister president

Adams (*to audience*) three a.m. – hume and trimble are
taking a break from negotiation

Trimble you going to tell adams now what we've just
decided

Hume david stop – we'll take a fifteen minute break

Trimble so you can go and tell adams

Hume grow up

Trimble this is another thing john i want to make clear –
i know what you are all at – keeping everyone up
all night is a tactic

Hume a tactic

Trimble yes – you want to get me exhausted so my resolve
weakens and i agree to something that i wouldn't
in the cold light of day

Hume	we're all tired
Trimble	you all take naps – i don't
Hume	you're right actually that's it – we all had a meeting – it was the get trimble exhausted and he'll agree to everything meeting – actually we gave it a name . . .
Adams	(*to audience – from table*) the get trimble exhausted and he'll agree to everything meeting
Hume	it's the get trimble exhausted and . . .
Trimble	very funny – just to let you know it's not working
Hume	i'll have to think of something else
Trimble	you do that
Hume	fifteen minutes
Trimble	fifteen minutes
	Hume walks to his chair and sits, head in hands. Trimble closes his eyes and dozes off. Adams coughs. Hume looks up at him and points to Trimble sleeping.
Adams	(*to audience*) four thirty a.m. – clinton makes some calls
Clinton	(*voice-over*) david – david
	Trimble remains asleep.
	Dialling.
	gerry
Adams	mister president
Clinton	(*voice-over*) how are things going gerry
Adams	fine mister president – i'm having problems getting to talk with tony at the moment – he seems to be concentrating on the unionists – i'm not happy about that

Clinton	(*voice-over*) one step at a time gerry – it's a difficult balancing act – you haven't been forgotten – i wouldn't let that happen – it's just about timing – the point is gerry you have to stick with it – i will be available from now until the end – the one thing you can't do gerry is walk – it's too close – we're too close

Dialling.

	john how are you – is it all coming together
Hume	slowly mister president
Clinton	(*voice-over*) good john good – do you see any problems – difficulties – that i can maybe help with
Hume	if you spoke to gerry it would help
Clinton	(*voice-over*) i have already john – we're getting to the last stages john everybody has to hold their nerve
Hume	trimble and adams are both getting edgy
Clinton	(*voice-over*) keep moving forward john
Hume	have a word with blair – he's getting a bit crazy – one minute he's full of beans because he thinks it's all coming together the next he's convinced it's all going to collapse
Clinton	(*voice-over*) i will – i will talk to him – do you think it will all collapse john
Hume	no
Clinton	(*voice-over*) no
Hume	we're too far down the road whoever walks away now will be blamed for the failure of a peace process – arguments are still to be had though
Clinton	(*voice-over*) there's always arguments john

Dialling.

david – david

Trimble wakes up and realises who it is on the phone.

Trimble   shit

Clinton   (*voice-over*) david

Trimble   mister president

Clinton   (*voice-over*) i phoned earlier

Trimble   sorry mister president i was . . .

Clinton   (*voice-over*) exhausted

Trimble   busy

Clinton   (*voice-over*) how are things going

Trimble   as expected

Clinton   (*voice-over*) you have my support

Trimble   regarding what mister president

Clinton   (*voice-over*) the success of the talks – i am a friend to both nationalism and unionism

Trimble   is that possible mister president

Clinton   (*voice-over*) resolution is always possible

Trimble   yes mister president – i appreciate your time and effort

Clinton   (*voice-over*) my door is always open david – so to speak – good luck

Trimble   thank you mister president – (*To audience.*) thank you mister president – i never know what to make of all that – necessary but unwanted – that's the situation i'm in and have been from the start

/

76

He sits in silence for a few moments.

Clinton (*voice-over, to audience*) five a.m. – no one is exactly sure how but it looks like a deal is slowly coming together – once it looked like things were coming together a bit of panic set in – they thought it actually might happen and got a bit nervy – then this happened

Mowlam bursts into Blair's office. She is speechless. Adams, Hume and Trimble watch the following scene from a distance.

Blair just say it

Mowlam trimble and the unionists want us to knock down murrayfield

Blair murrayfield – the home of scottish rugby

Mowlam yes murrayfield the home of scottish rugby

Hume (*to Adams*) trimble wants the british to knock down murrayfield

Adams (*to Hume*) the home of scottish rugby

Hume yes

Adams right – maybe he had a bad experience playing

Hume it is a sport connected with bad injuries

Adams i was expecting something but not this

Hume yeah – i thought maybe more marching

Adams i thought more marching

Hume well there you go

Blair why the fuck do they want that

Mowlam no idea

Blair could we even do that

Mowlam   what demolish an international rugby ground because the ulster unionists demand it as part of this agreement – no we fucking can't

Blair   does it have to be murrayfield – can it be some other rugby ground

Mowlam   what other rugby ground

Blair   i don't fucking know – i thought rugby over here was protestant – is it an anti scottish thing

Mowlam   we can negotiate – we'll say we can't do murrayfield but we can knock down somewhere else

Blair   get someone to draw up a list of rugby grounds the unionists would like demolished and we'll see if – fuck i don't know what we'll see

Mowlam   is there any rugby ground we want demolished and we could talk them round to demolishing that

Blair   are we dreaming this

She punches him in the stomach.

no

They laugh. Her harder than him.

this could only happen here

Mowlam   i know

Blair   we have negotiated our socks off

Mowlam   this has taken years

Blair   years – although the last few days have been the most important – everybody has given everything to try and secure a peaceful future for the peoples of these islands – the effort has been both heroic and historic and just as it looks like the whole

thing is coming together the whole fucking thing
is going to collapse because we won't be able to
demolish murrayfield the home of scottish rugby

Mowlam i wonder if we spoke to gerry would they blow
it up

*Trimble whispers to Mowlam then walks back to
his desk.*

maryfield – the government building where the
anglo irish agreement of 1985 was signed by
margaret thatcher and garret fitzgerald – the thing
that unionists hate more than anything

yes

Blair right

Hume (*to Adams*) did you hear that

Adams jesus christ

Mitchell hands out more documents.

Mitchell (*to audience*) this is it – the agreement – two years
in the making – endless toing and froing –
sleepless days and nights – one step forward and
twenty back et cetera et cetera et cetera – a thing
to be considered – hume wants it accepted so we
can move on – adams will consider with a view to
recommending – he is settled because blair said he
would talk again in a few weeks and keep the
channels of communication open – trimble – who
again has to be said is under a lot of pressure
from those behind him – is not what you could
consider pleased

The document is studied.

Trimble this is completely unacceptable prime minister

Blair you've read it

Trimble	of course i've read it
Blair	you got what you wanted – is that right
Trimble	i know but . . .
Blair	articles two and three of the irish constitution removed – you have your assembly and you limited the amount of cross border institutions
Trimble	i know but . . .
Blair	but nothing – i want to hear you say regarding those elements of the agreement you got what you wanted
Trimble	i know prime minister but . . .
Blair	say it – unless you start off this conversation with you agreeing with me that you got what you wanted regarding the things i've just mentioned you can leave and close the door behind you
Trimble	prime minister you don't understand . . .
Blair	say it
Trimble	. . .
Blair	say it
Trimble	we got what we wanted regarding the things you've just mentioned
Blair	right – so
Trimble	this is about decommissioning and prisoner release
Blair	yes
Trimble	what we have in this document is unacceptable – it needs changed
Blair	the document is the document – nothing can be changed now

Trimble   i don't understand – this will fail unless . . .

Blair   nothing can be changed david – this is what we're going with

Trimble   so you're happy with everything in this

Blair   i didn't say that – i said it can't be changed

Trimble   what am i going to do

Blair   try and get it through

Trimble   i won't be able to there'll be too much opposition to this – the future of the ruc – the relationship with dublin – nationalists holding a veto – and sinn fein ministers – all of that and then nothing on decommissioning and prisoners

Blair   not nothing

Trimble   i can't go into the meeting with that – we have no recourse – let adams and his like in and see what happens – prime minister i can't – i just know what's going to happen

Blair   try

Trimble   right – very good prime minister

As Trimble exits Mowlam enters. They pass in silence.

Mowlam   (*to audience*) david

Trimble   (*to audience*) secretary of state

Blair   he says it won't go through

Mowlam   that was always a possibility tony

Blair   he's right – there should be pressure applied

Mowlam   did you indicate that to him

Blair   more or less

Mowlam more or less

Blair this whole fucking thing is going to fall apart

Mowlam maybe there's another way of communicating to him – something more concrete

Ahern (*to audience*) moments – situations change in moments – trimble's at a meeting with the rest of his fellow unionists – it could go either way – walk or see it through to the end – all that time – all those words – all the what might have beens – the new horizons ahead – all put on hold – for god knows how long – if trimble walks –

The stage is silent – motionless.

moments – we all have them – the trick is to see them – tony decided to write trimble a letter

Blair i'll write him a letter

Ahern (*to audience*) none of the rest of us were meant to know that by the way – not that that matters – it's politics

Mowlam saying

Ahern (*to audience*) i'll agree with him

Blair i'll agree with him – i'll fucking agree with him – i'll say sinn fein will be excluded from the assembly if they haven't decommissioned by whatever time – i don't know – why didn't i think of that before – fucking agree with him

Blair gives Mitchell a letter who in turn gives it to Trimble.

Mitchell (*to audience*) the timing of this was close – it wasn't going trimble's way

Mumbled arguments/shouting fill the air. A table is banged. Silence.

Trimble reads the letter. Blair paces.

Trimble   (*to audience*) i understand your problem with paragraph twenty-five of strand one is that it requires decisions on those who should be excluded or removed from office in the northern ireland executive to be taken on a cross community basis – this letter is to let you know that if – during the course of the first six months of the shadow assembly or the assembly itself – these provisions having been shown to be ineffective – we shall support changes to these provisions to enable them to be made properly effective . . .

Blair indicates that he needs to wind up.

. . . is that the process of decommissioning should begin straightaway

Blair   (*to audience*) four forty p.m. – trimble calls mitchell

Everyone listens in.

Mitchell   hello david

Trimble   hello george

Mitchell   how's it going

Trimble   we're ready

Mitchell   are you alright

Trimble   we are ready to do business

Mitchell   that's great – congratulations

Trimble   thank you

Mitchell   i'd like to call a meeting as soon as possible – can you be ready in fifteen minutes

Trimble   yes

Mitchell	i'd like it to be a short meeting – no long speeches – everyone can talk as long as they want afterward
Trimble	that's fine by me
Mitchell	i'll see you in five

Mitchell exhausted falls asleep. Everyone starts making themselves presentable. Mowlam gathers up whatever copies of the agreement there are lying about and puts them with the rest. Blair throws a tablecloth over the books and this becomes a table. Everyone – except for Mitchell – lifts their chairs and sit around the table. Mitchell wakes up and quickly brings his chair to the table. He sits. They pose. A flash. A picture is taken.

are we agreed

Blair	yes
Mitchell	are we agreed
Ahern	yes
Mitchell	are we agreed
Trimble	yes
Mitchell	are we agreed
Hume	yes
Mitchell	are we agreed
Adams	i will bring it to our ard chomhairle in a positive manner
Mitchell	five twenty-six p.m. – these talks are adjourned – sine die

Mitchell, Blair and Ahern pose for a photo.

Blair	(*to audience*) this is the choice that humanity has to make in every age – between the daring that crosses new frontiers and allows us to make

progress or the timidity that shuts itself away in
seclusion where we stagnate – i believe that
courage has triumphed

Ahern   (*to audience*) and today's historic agreement
marks a new beginning for us all in northern
ireland and on the island of ireland – and in these
islands – it's a day we shall treasure – a day when
agreement and accommodation have taken the
place of difference in division – and today is
about the promise of a bright future – a day when
we hope a line can be drawn under the bloody
past – we must seize the opportunity

Blair and Ahern exit.

Trimble   (*to audience*) i look forward to the future – i hope
that the people of northern ireland will endorse
this agreement – i hope that we will be able to
move forward – forward together in a positive
way – i see a great opportunity there for us to
start a healing process in northern ireland

Adams   (*to audience*) there is much in this agreement but
there is still much to be done – the equality
agenda is paramount – the agreement has to bring
about parity of esteem equality of treatment and
equality of opportunity for all citizens in all
aspects of society

Hume   (*to audience*) peace created a space for these talks
which have now concluded with agreement – hope
for the future and what must be the determination
to maintain the agreement – we have a new dawn

Hume, Adams and Trimble exit.

Mowlam   (*to audience*) the last weather report – over the
next hour and only a few miles away a final
meteorological fitfulness of gusts drizzle sun
showers – and of course – snow

Mowlam and Mitchell are left on stage.

thank you

Mitchell   you take care

Mowlam exits.

(*to audience*) this agreement proves that democracy works – and in its wake we can say to the men of violence – to those who disdain democracy – whose tools are bombs and bullets – your way is not the right way – you will never solve the problems of northern ireland by violence – you will only make them worse – it doesn't take courage to shoot a policeman in the back of the head or to murder an unarmed taxi driver – what takes courage is to compete in the arena of democracy where the tools are persuasion fairness and common decency – you should help to build a society instead of tearing it apart – this agreement points the way

He leaves the stage. A few moments later the lights go out.